CLARE'S
CUPCAKE
CAFE

Menu

Hey There.

Clare Crespo

Photographs by Eric Staudenmaier

Cupcake!

35 Yummy Fun Cupcake Recipes for All Occasions

MELCHER
MEDIA

Let me tell you a little something about cupcakes: They are perfect. They are sweet, cheerful, fun, and their individual goodness makes you feel special. They can be romantic, or funny, or crazy, or just really cute. A cupcake can make people smile, and that's a pretty powerful move for a tiny baked good! Here are a few hot tips to make your cupcake creating a little easier.

1. BEFORE YOU START BAKING, lay out and measure all of your ingredients and decorating supplies. Baking cakes works better if ingredients are at room temperature, so items are easier to mix. You are also less likely to forget something if everything is laid out and ready to go!

2. FOLLOW CAKE RECIPES CLOSELY, and they will be way more likely to give good results. Save all of your creativity and experimentation for the decorations. That's where you can be a mad scientist!

3. BUY SOME PROPER FOOD COLORING. Cake and restaurant supply stores sell kits of gel food coloring in all sorts of beautiful colors. These are far superior to the ones you can get at the grocery store, because the colors are so much better. They will change your cupcake coloring life.

4. TAKE SHORTCUTS. If you are short on time (or patience!) but you really want to make some crazy cupcakes, use a cake mix. It may not be homemade, but it's still special that you took the time to make cupcakes, and your friends will still enjoy them! While you are at it, use some canned frosting, too. You can also bake cupcakes a day or two in advance. Just store them in an airtight container or some plastic wrap or foil.

5. MAKE THE CUPCAKES YOUR OWN. If you have a favorite cake recipe, by all means use it. And if you have a new idea for any of the recipes in this book, go for it. Adding your flair to a recipe will be rewarding, and I encourage it! I am not the cupcake boss—I only want to inspire you to love making cupcakes.

6. IF YOU GET TIRED after you have started a recipe, feel free to make a few special cupcakes and frost the others more simply. Display the "fancy" ones in the center of a platter and place the others around them. People may fight for the fancy ones, but you can assure them that they all taste delicious!

7. ALTERNATE FROSTING TECHNIQUE #1: To make a perfect frosted cupcake, use a pastry bag with a large tip, or just the coupler (the plastic tip holder). Squeeze the frosting onto the cupcake in a spiral string at the outer edge of the cupcake, twisting towards the center. Use a butter knife or a frosting spatula to smooth the edges of the spiral. Dip the knife in a bowl of warm water in between cupcakes.

8. ALTERNATE FROSTING TECHNIQUE #2: Take an unfrosted cupcake and dunk the top in a bowl of frosting. Twist it around to ensure that frosting covers the cake and pull it up. This is pretty fun and really easy to do.

9. UNFROSTED CUPCAKES FREEZE WELL. If you have some extra ones from a recipe or if you are really organized and planning ahead, just put them in a freezer bag and pop them in the freezer. It's exciting to know you have cupcakes in the freezer at any time just in case of a cupcake emergency!

10. TRAVELING WITH CUPCAKES can be tricky. They like to party in a car and make a mess of their frosting. Tupperware makes cool cupcake holders with little barriers around each cupcake. I like to lay down a couple of layers of paper towels flat in a box (plastic, foil, or cardboard) and place the cupcakes on top of it, which helps to prevent them from sliding around so much. I also place the cupcakes fairly close to each other, which stops them from rolling around if they slip.

Now you are ready to get in the kitchen and make some funny little masterpieces. Open your mind and have a great time! And just a reminder: You should always make sure you have a grown-up around when you are using tools like the stove and knives. Welcome to the wild world of cupcakes!

Contents

Use these master recipes to make the cupcakes in this book. Each recipe makes approximately 14-18 cupcakes.

Candy Dough

INGREDIENTS

4 tablespoons **evaporated milk**
½ teaspoon **vanilla extract**
4½ cups **powdered sugar**

METHOD

In a large bowl, gently mix together the evaporated milk, vanilla, and powdered sugar with a fork. When the mixture becomes too thick to stir, use your hands to knead it until it's smooth and easy to handle, adding more evaporated milk if necessary.

Chocolate Cupcakes

INGREDIENTS

3 ounces **unsweetened chocolate**
2 cups **all-purpose flour**
1 teaspoon **baking soda**
1 teaspoon **salt**
1½ cups **sugar**
⅓ cup **unsalted butter,** softened
1 cup **sour cream**
2 **eggs**
1 teaspoon **vanilla extract**
¼ cup hot **water**

METHOD

1. Preheat the oven to 350° F. Prepare cupcake tins as directed in the recipe you are following.

2. In a double boiler (or a microwave oven), melt the chocolate.

3. Sift the flour, baking soda, salt, and sugar together into a large mixing bowl.

4. To the flour mixture, add the butter and sour cream and beat well.

5. Stir in the melted chocolate.

6. Add the eggs, one at a time, and beat well after each addition.

7. Add the vanilla and hot water, and beat until the batter is smooth.

8. Pour the batter into the cupcake tins. Bake for 15 to 20 minutes, until the cake springs back when touched.

9. Remove from the oven and let cool for about 10 minutes, then turn the cupcakes out of the tins and onto a rack to finish cooling completely.

Chocolate-Caramel Cupcakes

INGREDIENTS

8 (2.05-ounce) **Milky Way candy bars**
1½ cups **unsalted butter**
2½ cups **all-purpose flour**
¼ teaspoon **baking soda**
¼ teaspoon **salt**
2 cups **sugar**
4 **eggs**
1¼ cups **buttermilk**
1 teaspoon **vanilla extract**
1 cup **pecans,** chopped

METHOD

1. Preheat the oven to 350° F. Prepare cupcake tins as directed in the recipe you are following.

2. In a double boiler, melt the candy bars together with ½ cup of the butter. Remove from heat and let cool.

3. Sift the flour, baking soda, and salt together into a large bowl.

4. In a separate bowl, cream the remaining 1 cup butter. Gradually add the sugar, creaming until light and fluffy.

5. Add the eggs, one at a time, beating well after each addition.

6. Add the melted candy bar mixture.

7. In a small bowl, combine the buttermilk and the vanilla.

8. To the candy bar mixture, add about ¼ of the flour mixture, then ¼ of the buttermilk mixture, and mix well. Continue alternating the remaining mixtures.

9. Stir in the pecans.

10. Pour the batter into the cupcake tins. Bake for 15 to 20 minutes, until the cake springs back when touched.

11. Remove from the oven and let cool for about 10 minutes, then turn the cupcakes out of the tins and onto a rack to finish cooling completely.

Cola Cupcakes

INGREDIENTS

1 cup **cola**
½ cup **semisweet chocolate chips**
2 cups **all-purpose flour,** sifted
1 cup **granulated sugar**
1 cup **dark brown sugar**
1 cup **cocoa powder**
1½ teaspoons **baking soda**
1 teaspoon **salt**
2 **eggs,** beaten
1 cup **buttermilk**
1 cup **vegetable oil**
1½ teaspoons **vanilla extract**

METHOD

1. Preheat oven the to 350° F. Prepare cupcake tins as directed in the recipe you are following.

2. Pour the cola and chocolate chips into a saucepan. Place over low heat, stirring often, until the chocolate chips are just melted. Let cool.

3. Sift the flour, sugar, brown sugar, cocoa, baking soda, and salt together into a medium mixing bowl.

4. In a large bowl, with an electric mixer, combine the eggs, buttermilk, oil, and vanilla.

5. With the mixer on, slowly add the cola mixture and mix well.

6. Gradually add the flour mixture and beat well.

7. Pour the batter into the cupcake tins. Bake for 15 to 20 minutes, until the cake springs back when touched.

8. Remove from the oven and let cool for about 10 minutes, then turn the cupcakes out of the tins and onto a rack to finish cooling completely.

Citrus Cupcakes

INGREDIENTS

3 cups **all-purpose flour**
1 teaspoon **baking powder**
1 teaspoon **baking soda**
Pinch of **salt**
1 cup **unsalted butter,** softened
1 cup **sugar**
2 **eggs**
¾ cup **buttermilk**
¾ cup **fresh citrus juice**
3 tablespoons **grated citrus zest** (orange, lemon, grapefruit, lime)

METHOD

1. Preheat the oven to 375° F. Prepare cupcake tins as directed in the recipe you are following.

2. Sift the flour, baking powder, baking soda, and salt together into a large bowl.

3. In a separate bowl, cream the butter. Gradually add the sugar to the butter, and cream together until light and fluffy.

4. To the butter mixture, add the eggs, one at a time, and beat well after each addition.

5. In a small bowl, combine the buttermilk, citrus juice, and zest.

6. To the butter mixture, add about one quarter of the flour mixture and mix well. Add about one quarter of the buttermilk mixture and mix well. Continue alternating the flour mixture and buttermilk mixture, beating after each addition until smooth.

7. Pour the batter into the cupcake tins. Bake for 15 to 20 minutes, until the cake springs back when touched.

8. Remove from the oven and let cool for about 10 minutes, then turn the cupcakes out of the tins and onto a rack to finish cooling completely.

Honey Cupcakes

INGREDIENTS

2½ cups **all-purpose flour**
3 teaspoons **baking powder**
½ teaspoon **salt**
⅓ cup **unsalted butter,** softened
½ cup **sugar**
½ cup **honey**
1 **egg**
1 cup **whole milk**
1 teaspoon **vanilla extract**

METHOD

1. Preheat the oven to 350° F. Prepare cupcake tins as directed in the recipe you are following.

2. Sift the flour, baking powder, and salt together into a large mixing bowl.

3. Put the butter in a separate bowl and gradually add the sugar and honey, creaming until light and fluffy.

4. Add the egg and beat thoroughly.

5. In a small bowl, combine the milk and vanilla.

6. To the butter mixture, add about one quarter of the flour mixture and mix well. Add about one quarter of the milk mixture and mix well. Continue alternating the flour mixture and milk mixture, beating after each addition until smooth.

7. Pour the batter into the cupcake tins. Bake for 15 to 20 minutes, until the cake springs back when touched.

8. Remove from the oven and let cool for about 10 minutes, then turn the cupcakes out of the tins and onto a rack to finish cooling completely.

Mocha Cupcakes

INGREDIENTS

1⅓ cups **all-purpose flour,** sifted
1 teaspoon **baking powder**
½ teaspoon **baking soda**
¼ teaspoon **salt**
½ cup **cocoa powder**
½ cup **unsalted butter,** softened
1 cup **sugar**
1 **egg**
½ cup **whole milk**
½ cup strongly **brewed coffee,** cooled
1 teaspoon **vanilla extract**

METHOD

1. Preheat the oven to 350° F. Prepare cupcake tins as directed in the recipe you are following.

2. Sift the flour, baking powder, baking soda, salt, and cocoa powder together into a large mixing bowl.

3. In a separate bowl, cream the butter together with the sugar until light and fluffy.

4. Add the egg and mix well.

5. In a small bowl, combine the milk, coffee, and vanilla.

6. To the butter mixture, add about one quarter of the flour mixture and mix well. Add about one quarter of the milk mixture and mix well. Continue alternating the flour mixture and milk mixture, beating after each addition until smooth.

7. Pour the batter into the cupcake tins. Bake for 15 to 20 minutes, until the cake springs back when touched.

8. Remove from the oven and let cool for about 10 minutes, then turn the cupcakes out of the tins and onto a rack to finish cooling completely.

Peanut Butter Cupcakes

INGREDIENTS

1¾ cups **all-purpose flour**
3 teaspoons **baking powder**
½ teaspoon **salt**
⅓ cup **unsalted butter,** softened
1¼ cups firmly packed **light brown sugar**
2 **eggs**
⅓ cup **salted peanut butter,** crunchy or smooth
1 cup **whole milk**
1 teaspoon **vanilla extract**

METHOD

1. Preheat the oven to 350° F. Prepare cupcake tins as directed in the recipe you are following.

2. Sift the flour, baking powder, and salt together into a large bowl.

3. In a separate bowl, cream the butter together with the brown sugar.

4. Add the eggs, one at a time, and beat after each addition until light and fluffy.

5. Add the peanut butter and mix well.

6. In a small bowl, combine the milk and vanilla.

7. To the butter mixture, add about one quarter of the flour mixture and mix well. Add about one quarter of the milk mixture and mix well. Continue alternating the flour mixture and milk mixture, beating after each addition until smooth.

8. Pour the batter into the cupcake tins. Bake for 18 to 23 minutes, until the cake springs back when touched.

9. Remove from the oven and let cool for about 10 minutes, then turn the cupcakes out of the tins and onto a rack to finish cooling completely.

Pineapple Cupcakes

INGREDIENTS

2¼ cups **all-purpose flour**
2 cups **sugar**
2 teaspoons **baking soda**
½ teaspoon **salt**
2 **eggs,** beaten
¼ cup **vegetable oil**
1 teaspoon **vanilla extract**
1 (20-ounce) can **crushed pineapple with juice**

METHOD

1. Preheat the oven to 350° F. Prepare cupcake tins as directed in the recipe you are following.

2. In a large bowl, mix together the flour, sugar, baking soda, and salt.

3. Add the eggs, oil, and vanilla and mix well.

4. Add the pineapple and juice and mix well.

5. Fill the cupcake tins two-thirds full with the batter. Bake for 15 to 20 minutes, until the cake springs back when touched.

6. Remove from the oven and let cool for about 10 minutes, then turn the cupcakes out of the tins and onto a rack to finish cooling completely.

Red Velvet Cupcakes

INGREDIENTS

2½ cups **all-purpose flour**
1 teaspoon **salt**
½ cup **unsalted butter,** softened
1½ cups **sugar**
2 **eggs**
2 tablespoons **cocoa powder**
2 ounces **water**
2 ounces **red food coloring**
1 cup **buttermilk**
1 teaspoon **vanilla extract**
1 teaspoon **white vinegar**
1 teaspoon **baking soda**

METHOD

1. Preheat the oven to 350° F. Prepare cupcake tins as directed in the recipe you are following.

2. Cream butter and sugar until fluffy.

3. Add eggs and blend well.

4. Make a paste of cocoa and food coloring and add to the butter mixture.

5. Sift flour and salt together into this mixture.

6. One at a time, add the following ingredients: buttermilk, vanilla, and water.

7. In a small bowl, combine the vinegar and the baking soda. Fold it into the cake batter. Make sure it's incorporated, but don't beat it.

8. Pour the batter into the cupcake tins. Bake for 15 to 20 minutes, until the cake springs back when touched.

9. Remove from oven and let cool for about 10 minutes, then turn the cupcakes out of the tins and onto a rack to finish cooling completely.

White Cupcakes

INGREDIENTS

3 cups **all-purpose flour**
2½ teaspoons **baking powder**
½ teaspoon **salt**
⅔ cup **unsalted butter,** softened
1¾ cups **sugar**
2 **eggs**
1¼ cups **whole milk**
1 teaspoon **vanilla extract**

METHOD

1. Preheat the oven to 350° F. Prepare cupcake tins as directed in the recipe you are following.

2. Sift the flour, baking powder, and salt together into a medium bowl.

3. In a separate, larger bowl, cream the butter. Gradually add the sugar, creaming until light and fluffy.

4. Add the eggs one at a time, and beat well after each addition.

5. In a small bowl, combine the milk and vanilla.

6. To the butter mixture, add about one quarter of the flour mixture and mix well. Add about one quarter of the milk mixture and mix well. Continue alternating the flour mixture and milk mixture, beating after each addition until smooth.

7. Pour the batter into the cupcake tins. Bake for 15 to 20 minutes, until the cake springs back when touched.

8. Remove from the oven and let cool for about 10 minutes, then turn the cupcakes out of the tins and and onto a rack to finish cooling completely.

Chocolate Butter Cream Frosting

INGREDIENTS

4 cups **powdered sugar**
¾ cup **cocoa powder**
½ cup **unsalted butter,** softened
½ teaspoon **salt**
⅓ cup **whole milk,** or more if necessary
1 teaspoon **vanilla extract**

METHOD

1. Sift the powdered sugar and cocoa powder together into a bowl.

2. In another large bowl, cream the butter until smooth.

3. Add the powdered sugar and cocoa powder, salt, milk, and vanilla and mix until smooth and creamy. Add 1 to 2 more tablespoons milk if the consistency is too thick.

Cream Cheese Frosting

INGREDIENTS

1 (8-ounce) package **cream cheese,** softened
½ cup **unsalted butter,** softened
1½ cups powdered **sugar**
1 teaspoon **vanilla extract**

METHOD

Blend all the ingredients together until smooth.

Fluffy Frosting

INGREDIENTS

1 cup **whole milk**
6 tablespoons **all-purpose flour**
1 cup **unsalted butter,** softened
1½ cups **powdered sugar,** sifted
1 teaspoon **vanilla extract**

METHOD

1. In a saucepan, whisk the milk and flour until the mixture is very smooth. Bring to a boil over medium heat and boil for 1 minute, stirring constantly. Remove from the heat and let cool.

2. With an electric mixer, beat the butter, powdered sugar, and vanilla together for a couple of minutes, until light and fluffy. Add the cooled milk mixture and continue beating for a few more minutes, until the frosting is soft, light, and fluffy.

Royal Icing

INGREDIENTS

2 **egg whites***
3 cups **powdered sugar**
1 teaspoon **fresh lemon juice**
¼ teaspoon **salt**

METHOD

Combine all of the ingredients in a large grease-free bowl. With an electric mixer, beat at high speed for several minutes, until the icing holds soft peaks.

*Some folks don't think that eating raw egg whites is a good idea. If you are one of them, you can get premade royal icing at a cake decorating store or just mix the powdered sugar, lemon juice, and 1 to 2 tablespoons water together.

Vanilla Butter Cream Frosting

INGREDIENTS

½ cup **unsalted butter,** softened
4 cups **powdered sugar**
½ teaspoon **salt**
⅓ cup **whole milk**
1 teaspoon **vanilla extract**

METHOD

1. In a large bowl, cream the butter until smooth.

2. Add the powdered sugar, salt, milk, and vanilla and mix until smooth and creamy.

White Ganache

INGREDIENTS

1 (12-ounce) bag **white chocolate chips**
1 cup **heavy cream**
1 tablespoon **unsalted butter**

METHOD

1. Put the white chocolate chips in a stainless-steel bowl. In a saucepan, heat the cream over medium heat until it boils. Add the cream to the white chocolate and whisk until melted. Add the butter and keep whisking until smooth.

2. Place the bowl in the fridge until the ganache is cool and thick. Pour over cupcakes.

9

You know that saying "You have to learn the rules before you can break them"? Well, here you go. Master this recipe and the cupcake world is your cupcake oyster! After making these, you will truly understand the art of the cupcake. This recipe makes that quintessential cupcake. This is the cupcake I dream about. This is the cupcake I draw on my notebooks. This is the cupcake I want to be!

In the grand museum of baking, one item alone is worthy of our utmost reverence and respect. Behold, it is the awe-inspiring Classic Cupcake.

Classic Cupcake

INGREDIENTS

1 recipe batter for **White Cupcakes** (page 8)
White cupcake liners

METHOD

Line cupcake tins with paper liners. Fill the liners two-thirds full with batter and bake the cupcakes as directed in the recipe.

Classic Icing

INGREDIENTS

1 recipe **Vanilla Butter Cream Frosting** (page 9)
Pink food coloring
Maraschino cherries with stems

METHOD

1. Add a few drops of pink food coloring to the frosting and mix well.

2. Frost the cupcakes with reverence and respect.

3. Place one cherry in the center of each cupcake.

4. Now stand quietly and observe the awe-inspiring beauty of the cupcakes you've created.

Classic Cupcake

CLASSIC CUPCAKE

Aspirin Cupcakes

1 recipe **batter for any cupcake**
(whatever you feel like today!)
1½ cups **fruit jam**
Powdered sugar
1 (24-ounce) package **premade rolled fondant**
(available at specialty pastry stores or online)

Take two of these and call me in the morning—I bet you'll feel a whole lot better!

METHOD

1. Grease and flour cupcake tins. Fill the tins halfway full with batter and bake the cupcakes as directed in the recipe.

2. "Frost" the cupcakes with the jam.

3. Sprinkle powdered sugar on the work surface and use a rolling pin to roll out the fondant to about ⅛ inch thick. Cut the fondant into 4-inch squares. Drape a square over a cupcake. Smooth the fondant down with your hand, getting rid of air bubbles and creases. With a small sharp knife, cut away the excess fondant around the bottom edge. Continue with the rest of the cupcakes. Make a ball with the scraps and roll it out again for more fondant squares.

4. Using the back of a butter knife, make an indentation across the center of each cupcake to make it resemble an aspirin. If you have a little patience, use a small not-so-sharp knife and press the word aspirin into the fondant.

Make these pain-killing cupcakes for your friend with the sprained ankle.

12

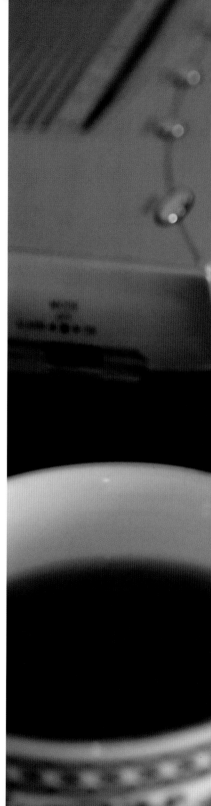

Astrology Cupcakes

What's your sign? Use these cupcakes to ask your friends at your next party.

INGREDIENTS

A few sheets of **paper** and a **pen**
Tinfoil
1 recipe **batter for any cupcake**
(whatever seems delicious to you today!)
1 recipe **Vanilla Butter Cream Frosting** (page 9)
Food coloring (whatever colors remind you of the zodiac—purple and teal and magenta work for me!)
Small candies to "write" with or **decorative frosting** in a different color than your cupcakes

METHOD

1. Line cupcake tins with paper or foil liners. Cut one sheet of paper into 12 pieces. Write a sign of the zodiac on each piece and lay them in front of you in the order that they go in the year: **Capricorn, Aquarius, Pisces, Aries, Taurus, Gemini, Cancer, Leo, Virgo, Libra, Scorpio, Sagittarius.**

2. Cut another sheet of paper into 24 2-by-½-inch rectangles. Look at a newspaper, a magazine, or on the Internet to check out this month's horoscopes. Write a brief version of the horoscope on each rectangle. Make sure to write what zodiac sign it applies to on the back. Feel free to paraphrase the horoscopes, or make them funny, or maybe just use one good line on your versions. Write them out again so that you have enough horoscopes for your cupcakes. Place them in groups next to the piece of paper that says what sign they are so that you can keep them all straight.

3. Cut 24 4-by-2-inch pieces of tinfoil. Securely fold the tinfoil around each fortune and place them next to their sign again, to keep them straight.

4. Fill the cupcake liners two-thirds full with the batter. Securely wrap a little tinfoil around one corner of your cupcake tin. This will be your top left corner. From that corner, drop in the Capricorn horoscope; continue dropping in horoscopes in the order that they appear in the zodiac, from left to right.

5. Bake the cupcakes as directed in the recipe. When you remove them from the oven, and they have cooled in their tins, you can use the same system you did before, by taking them out one at a time from left to right and placing them next to their sign.

6. Tint the frosting with the food coloring of your choice. Frost the cupcakes, being careful that once they are frosted, they are placed next to their sign again.

7. Using the decorative candies or decorative frosting in a contrasting color, draw the sign of the zodiac on each cupcake.

Make sure that your guests know there's a fortune in each cupcake before they eat them!

These are good to make for a party for a few people with the same sign. You could have a Pisces Party and make Pisces cupcakes with different birthday horoscopes in each of them.

Capricorn

aquarius

Pisces

aries

Taurus

Gemini

♋︎ Cancer   ♌︎ Leo   ♍︎ Virgo   ♎︎ Libra   ♏︎ Scorpio   ♐︎ Sagittarius

Imagine the magical mittens you could knit with this yummy yarn!

INGREDIENTS

1 recipe **batter for any cupcake**
1 recipe **Vanilla Butter Cream Frosting** (page 9)
Food coloring
Pastry bag and **medium tip**

METHOD

1. Line cupcake tins with paper liners. Fill the liners two-thirds full with batter and bake the cupcakes as directed in the recipe.

2. Tint the frosting with the food coloring of your choice. Using a pastry bag and tip, pipe frosting onto the cupcake in lines across the cupcake. Apply the lines in different directions to make it look like a wound ball of yarn.

Use different colors of frosting to make a collection of various balls of yarn and serve them in a basket. How about making these the next time you invite your friends over to work on a knitting project?

Ball of Yarn Cupcakes

20 **glass marble**s or small balls of **tinfoil**
1 recipe batter for **White Cupcakes** (page 8)
2 to 3 cups **strawberry jelly** or **smooth strawberry jam**
1 recipe **Vanilla Butter Cream Frosting** (page 9)
Red and **blue food coloring**
Pastry bag and **medium round tip** (optional)

METHOD

1. Line cupcake tins with paper liners. Fill the liners two-thirds full with the batter. Place 1 marble or tinfoil ball between each liner and the tin. This will make a dent in your cupcake when it bakes to make it heart-shaped. Bake the cupcakes as directed in the recipe. If you are using marbles, be careful when removing the cupcakes from the tins because the marbles will be very hot.

2. With a small paring knife, cut out a circle about the size of a dime in the center of each cupcake, going about two thirds of the way in. Pull the little plug of cake out. Cut off the top of this piece (about ½ inch thick) and eat or discard the bottom. Use a teaspoon or a squeeze bottle to fill the hole partway with the strawberry jelly "blood." Put the little cake plug back in. Continue with the rest of the hearts.

3. Put one third of the frosting into two separate bowls. Color one bowl of frosting with the red food coloring. Tint the other bowl of frosting blue. Tint the remaining two thirds pink.

4. Frost the cupcakes with the pink frosting. Make it super smooth by dipping a butter or frosting/palette knife in a bowl of hot water and smoothing it over the top. With the pastry bag or a knife, use the red and blue frosting to make veins on the hearts.

Give a cupcake heart to the one you love on Valentine's Day.

> These cupcakes are heartbreakingly sweet.

Bleeding Heart Cupcakes

Brain Cupcakes

Only a mad scientist with a sweet tooth would dream of cooking up these brains in the laboratory.

INGREDIENTS

Pink or white paper cupcake liners
1 recipe batter for **Red Velvet Cupcakes** (page 8)
1 recipe **Vanilla Butter Cream Frosting** (page 9)
Red and **black food coloring**
Pastry bag and **large round tip**

METHOD

1. Line cupcake tins with the liners. Fill the cupcake liners two-thirds full with the batter and bake the cupcakes as directed in the recipe.

2. Mix a drop of red and a drop of black food coloring into the frosting to make it a pinkish gray brain color.

3. Using the pastry bag, pipe the frosting in a squiggly pile on half of each cupcake top (brains have two hemispheres, you know). Now pipe the frosting in a squiggly pile on the other half of the cupcake top.

Serve these smart cupcakes to celebrate acing a test. They're also ideal for a graduation party.

Buried Alive Cupcakes

> It might not be so bad to be buried alive in a delicious chocolate cupcake.

INGREDIENTS

1 recipe batter for **Chocolate Cupcakes** (page 6)
1 recipe **Chocolate Butter Cream Frosting** (page 9)
3 cups **chocolate cookie crumbs**
Small **plastic doll arms** (available at craft stores)
or you could mold arms out of **marzipan**

METHOD

1. Line cupcake tins with the liners. Fill the cupcake liners two-thirds full with the batter and bake the cupcakes as directed in the recipe.

2. Frost the cupcakes.

3. Sprinkle chocolate cookie crumbs on the frosting to the make the sacred dirt of your graveyard. Insert a plastic arm into the frosting. Repeat with the remaining cupcakes. Every cupcake doesn't have to have an arm. There can be plain dirt cupcakes in your spooky scene, too.

What better way to scare your friends on Halloween than with these scary cupcakes from beyond the grave. Boo!

R.I.P.
Fruit
Cake
1932 - 1968

Buttons and Thread Cupcakes

> Use these yummy sewing supplies to mend that magical sweater just like your grandmother would.

Buttons

INGREDIENTS

1 recipe **batter for any cupcake**

METHOD

1. Grease and flour cupcake tins. Fill the tins two-thirds full with the batter and bake the cupcakes as directed in the recipe.

2. Take half of the cupcakes and slice each one into three discs (including the tops). These will be your buttons.

3. With the remaining cupcakes, using a small serrated knife, carve the edge of the cupcake top to be flush with the base of the cupcake. You will end up with a small cylinder. These will become your spools of thread.

Buttons Icing

INGREDIENTS

1 recipe **Vanilla Butter Cream Frosting** (page 9), colored with the **food coloring of your choice**
1 stiff **plastic straw**

METHOD

1. Frost the tops and sides of the cupcake discs.

2. Using a straw, poke out 4 holes in each cupcake disc to make them resemble buttons.

Spool Construction

INGREDIENTS

3 (8-ounce) packages **super-long thin licorice** (red or black)
1 (24-ounce) package **premade rolled fondant** (available at specialty pastry stores or online)

METHOD

1. Place some of the strings of licorice in the microwave for 15 seconds to soften them and make them easier to wind around your cupcake.

2. Wind the licorice around the center of the cupcake cylinders, and tuck the ends under to secure. You may wish to frost the sides of the cylinders to make the licorice easier to adhere.

3. Roll out the fondant. Using a glass a little bit bigger than the cupcake cylinders or a small sharp knife, cut out two discs for each cupcake you intend to turn into a spool of thread. These will be the tops and bottoms of your spools.

4. Place a cupcake wound in licorice on top of one disc. Continue with the remaining cupcakes.

5. Using a straw or a small sharp knife, cut a small circle into the remaining candy discs. Place one disc on top of each cupcake to complete your spools.

You can make a needle for your sewing supplies by coloring a toothpick with a gray water-based marker.

Makes 20 buttons and 10 spools

INGREDIENTS

1 recipe batter for **Citrus Cupcakes** (page 7)
1 recipe **Vanilla Butter Cream Frosting**, adding
2 teaspoons **finely grated citrus rind** (page 9)
Yellow, green, or **orange jelly candies** or **gumdrops**
½ (12-ounce) package **premade rolled fondant**
(available at specialty pastry stores or online)
Yellow, green, or **orange food coloring**
White candy-covered sunflower seeds (optional)

METHOD

1. Decide whether you would like to make lime, lemon, or orange cupcakes. This will determine what citrus rind to grate into the batter and frosting and what color food coloring and jelly candies you will need.

2. Line cupcake tins with paper liners. Fill cupcake tins two-thirds full with the batter and bake the cupcakes as directed in the recipe.

3. Frost the cupcakes.

4. If your jelly candies are large (about an inch in diameter), cut them into triangles by slicing off two sides to make a point. If the candies are smaller, or if you are using gumdrops, use a rolling pin to spread them out a bit so that they will be large and flat enough to cut into triangles. Place these on the Butter Cream Frosting, points facing the center.

5. Knead a few drops of food coloring into the fondant to make it the color of a lime, lemon, or orange rind. Roll the fondant to about ¼ inch thickness. With a small sharp knife, slice ½-inch strips of fondant. Wrap the strips around the top edge of the cupcake, using a little water to join the ends together if necessary.

6. Using a little frosting as glue, stick a few white candy-covered sunflower seeds on top to look like seeds.

Make a little extra money this summer by selling these juicy cupcakes at an alternative lemonade stand.

27

PARIS

HONOLULU

LOS ANGELES

TOKYO

INGREDIENTS

1 recipe **batter for any cupcake**
1 recipe **Vanilla Butter Cream Frosting** (page 9)
Black and **red food coloring**
1 recipe **Royal Icing** (page 9)
Pastry bag and a **medium star or round tip**
plus a **very small round tip**
24 **small round candies**

METHOD

1. Line cupcake tins with paper liners. Fill the tins two-thirds full with the batter and bake the cupcakes as directed in the recipe.

2. Frost the cupcakes with the Vanilla Butter Cream Frosting, using a small butter knife or a frosting/palette knife dipped in hot water to smooth out the surface.

3. Tint the remaining frosting with a few drops of black frosting to make a gray color. With the pastry bag and the medium tip, pipe this around the edge of your cupcake to make the clock's rim.

4. Add red food coloring to one third of the Royal Icing. Add black food coloring to the remaining icing. With the pastry bag and very small tip, carefully write numbers around the face of the clock in black icing. (You may find it easier just to write the 12, 3, 6, and 9 and use short lines for the other numbers.) Draw in the hour and minute hands with the black icing. Now use the red icing and a pastry bag with the very small tip to pipe the second hand onto the faces of the clocks.

5. Place the small round candies into the centers of your clocks.

Have fun picking the times for your clocks. Serve 12:00 cupcakes to celebrate New Year's Eve. Or you could ice some with the kickoff time for the Super Bowl, the time you were born, or your favorite time of day.

It's always a good time for a cupcake!

Clock Cupcakes

29

1 recipe batter for **Mocha Cupcakes**
(page 7)
1 recipe **White Ganache**, adding
2 tablespoons **instant espresso powder**
to the cream while it heats (page 8)
10 **coffee cups**
Whipped cream (optional)

1. Grease and flour cupcake tins. Fill the tins two-thirds full with the batter and bake the cupcakes as directed in the recipe. While the cupcakes are baking, mix up the White Ganache.

2. Place a cupcake in a coffee cup. It is good if the cupcake fits snugly so that the ganache won't seep down into the cup. Depending on the height of the coffee cup you use, you may need to put 2 cup-cakes in each cup. If this is the case, spoon a little ganache in between the cupcakes. Spoon ganache over the top of the cupcakes.

3. Dab a little whipped cream on top, if you take your coffee with cream.

These would be good to make in the afternoon when you need a little pick-me-up. Serve with a spoon, as you would a cup of coffee.

Care to join me for a nice cup of joe?

Coffee Cup Cakes

> I bet you'd feel a whole lot richer if you found one of these coin cupcakes in the seat of your car.

Coin Cupcakes

INGREDIENTS

Gold and **silver foil cupcake liners**
1 recipe **batter for any cupcake** (whatever you feel like today!)
1 recipe **Royal Icing** (page 9)
Black, orange, and **brown food coloring**
Gold and **silver sparkly powder** (available at cake decorating stores)
Small clean **paintbrush**
Pastry bag and **very small round tip**

METHOD

1. Line cupcake tins with the liners. Fill the liners half full with the batter and bake the cupcakes as directed in the recipe.

2. If you are planning on making pennies, nickels, and dimes, separate the icing into three separate bowls. This would be a good time to take out a few coins from your wallet for reference. Use the orange and brown food coloring to make a copper color for your penny icing. Use the black food coloring to make a light gray for the dimes and a little darker gray for the nickels. Use the gold-lined cupcakes for the pennies and the silver-lined ones for the dimes and nickels. Place a spoonful of the icing on each cupcake and let it spread to the sides. Let the icing set. While you are waiting, cover the remaining icing with plastic wrap.

3. Using the pastry bag, pipe the same colored icing on the cupcakes in the design of the coins. Don't worry about getting every detail of the coin on the cupcakes-they don't have to be perfect! Just put a face in profile and maybe write "5¢." You'll get the point across. Continue with the rest of the cupcakes. Once the icing has set, brush the gold sparkly powder on the pennies and the silver sparkly powder on the nickels and dimes.

Serve these to celebrate Presidents' Day, the arrival of the tooth fairy, or a friend or family member's big promotion.

32

Cola
Cupcakes

It's a hot day, and you've been working so hard. How about taking a break with a nice can of cupcake cola? There's a sixer, so you can share with your buddies.

INGREDIENTS

1 recipe batter for **Cola Cupcakes** (page 6)
1 recipe **Vanilla Butter Cream Frosting,**
using 1/3 cup **cola** and 1/4 cup **cocoa powder**
in place of the milk (page 9)
1 (24-ounce) package **premade rolled fondant**
(available at specialty pastry stores or online)
Black food coloring
Food coloring for your cans (your pick!)
Powdered sugar
Small clean **paintbrush**
1 recipe **Royal Icing** (page 9)
Pastry bag and **small round tip**

METHOD

1. Grease and flour cupcake tins. Fill the tins two-thirds full with the batter and bake the cupcakes as directed in the recipe. When the cupcakes are completely cooled, trim the edges with a serrated knife so the cupcakes are more cylindrical. If the tops are domed, trim them to make them flatter.

2. Frost the top of a cupcake and stack another cupcake on top. Frost that cupcake, and stack another on top of that. Measure the height and width of your tower of cupcakes, and make a note of it. Now, using the Vanilla Butter Cream Frosting, frost the outside of the tower of cupcakes you've made. You don't have to be that neat about it, because this frosting is going to be covered. Continue with 5 more "cans."

3. Sprinkle a bit of powdered sugar on a work surface. Roll out a rectangle of fondant, about $1/8$–$1/4$ inch thick, that is about an inch taller than your tower and $1/2$ inch wider. Carefully wrap your tower with this rectangle. You can use a little water or a dab of Royal Icing to stick the seams together, flattening the top and bottom. With a brush, paint the label whatever color you choose. Paint the top and the bottom of the can gray. Continue with the remaining "cans."

4. With the pastry bag and tip, use the Royal Icing to make the lettering on your labels.

These are good to serve with burgers and chips while watching the game with your pals.

1 recipe **batter for any cupcake**

1 recipe **Vanilla Butter Cream Frosting**
(page 9)

Red food coloring

24 pairs **red gummy fish** or **cars**

1 (8-ounce) package **red whip licorice**

24 pairs **red gummy ants, worms,** or
jelly beans

24 pairs **small round candies** or **jelly
beans** (for eyes)

24 pairs **chocolate sprinkles** (for angry
eyebrows)

METHOD

1. Line the cupcake tins with paper
liners. Fill the liners two-thirds full
with the batter and bake the cupcakes as directed in the recipe.
When the cupcakes are completely
cooled, slice off the tops. Munch on
the cupcake bottoms now or save
them for another treat.

2. Tint the frosting with the food coloring to make a bright red color.
Frost the cupcake tops. Arrange
them on plates or a tray.

3. Cut a V out of a gummy fish or
car to make one of the front claws.
Continue with the rest of the
gummy fish or cars. Insert these
into the front side of each "crab."

4. Slice the whip licorice into 2-inch
pieces. Insert 3 pieces into each
side of each crab.

5. Insert gummy ants or jelly beans
into the back sides of your crab. If
you are using gummy worms, slice
them into 1-inch pieces before
inserting them.

6. To make your crabs come alive,
insert 2 round candies (or small jelly
bean halves) into the front of each
crab. Stick 1 chocolate sprinkle
above each eye for angry eyebrows.

You can serve these for dessert
at a crab boil or beach party.

> These crabs may look like
> they want to pinch you on
> the nose, but don't worry—
> they're really nice on the
> inside.

Crabcakes

Crop Circle
Cupcakes

INGREDIENTS

1 recipe batter for **Chocolate Cupcakes** (page 6)
1 recipe **Vanilla Butter Cream Frosting** (page 9)
Green food coloring
Pastry bag and **grass tip**
Small palette knife, chopstick, or **popsicle stick**
for scraping
Small plastic cows, tractors, or **farmers** (optional)

METHOD

1. Line cupcake tins with paper or foil liners.
Fill the liners two-thirds full with the batter and
bake the cupcakes as directed in the recipe.

2. Tint the frosting grass green with the food
coloring. Using the pastry bag, pipe green grass
all over the cupcakes. With the scraping tool,
carefully scrape away the frosting in a simple
geometric shape, exposing the chocolate cake
"earth" below. Continue making crop circles on
all of the cupcakes. Place the cows, tractors, and
farmers on the remaining green grass, if you wish.

Make these other-worldly cupcakes the next
time you have aliens over for dinner.

Who in the universe is making
those crazy crop circles? Could
it be creative aliens?
Mischievous farmers? A genius
mutant cow? The FBI? Could it
actually be YOU making crop
circles in your sleep? Maybe
you'll discover some clues to
this mysterious occurrence
by making these conspiracy
cupcakes.

Cubcake

INGREDIENTS

1 recipe **batter for any cupcakes**
1 recipe **Vanilla Butter Cream Frosting**

METHOD

Place cupcake liners in tins. Fill the tins two-thirds full with the batter and bake the cupcakes as directed in the recipe.

Panda Face

INGREDIENTS

Chocolate nonpareils for ears
Chocolate disc-shaped candies (like chocolate-covered mints) for circles around eyes
Small round chocolate candies (chocolate-covered peanuts, for example) for noses
White chocolate chips and **black decorating gel** or **black food coloring** for eyes, or **sugar eyes** (found at cake and candy decorating stores).

METHOD

1. Frost the cupcakes.

2. Place two chocolate disk candies on the top of the cupcake for ears. Place two more in the center for the dark circles around pandas' eyes. Place sugar "eyes" on these chocolate disks using a little frosting as glue. If you are using white chocolate chips, cut off the points and stick them onto the disks with a little frosting. Draw pupils on with a toothpick and a little black food coloring, or use a dot of black gel frosting. Stick a small round chocolate candy in the middle of the panda's face for the nose.

Koala Face

INGREDIENTS

Brown food coloring
Walnut halves for ears
White chocolate chips and **black decorating gel** or **black food coloring** for eyes, or **sugar eyes** (found at cake and candy decorating stores)
Chocolate-covered Brazil nuts or **almonds** for noses (if you can't find these separately, they are usually included in a "bridge mix")

METHOD

1. Tint the Vanilla Butter Cream Frosting with a little brown food coloring to make a tan color. Frost the cupcakes.

2. Place two walnut halves in the top of the cupcake for ears. Place two sugar eyes into the center of the cupcake. If you are using white chocolate chips, cut off the points and place them into the center of the cupcake. Draw pupils on with a toothpick and a little black food coloring, or use a dot of black gel frosting. Stick a chocolate-covered nut in the middle of the koala's face for the nose.

Brown Bear Face

INGREDIENTS

Brown food coloring
Chocolate disc-shaped candy (like chocolate-covered mints)
White chocolate chips and **black decorating gel** or **black food coloring** for eyes, or **sugar eyes** (found at cake and candy decorating stores)
Pink or **red jelly beans**

METHOD

1. Tint the Vanilla Butter Cream Frosting with brown food coloring, or use Chocolate Butter Cream Frosting. You can make the chocolate frosting darker with brown food coloring.

2. Frost the cupcakes.

3. Place two chocolate disc-shaped candies into top of cupcake for the ears. If the discs are large, cut off one third of the circle with a small knife and stick the remainder into the frosting. Place two sugar eyes into the center of the cupcake. If you are using white chocolate chips, cut off the points and place them into the center of the cupcake. Draw pupils on with a toothpick and a little black food coloring, or use a dot of black gel frosting. Place a jelly bean in the center of the cupcake for the brown bear's nose.

Make these for a springtime "No More Hibernation" party or a teddy bear picnic.

Who's peeking out of the trees? Why it's a fuzzy brown bear, rare panda, and shy koala cubcake!

Cubcakes

Cupcake for a Giant

INGREDIENTS

1 recipe **batter for any cupcake** (whatever strikes your fancy today!)
1 recipe **Vanilla** or **Chocolate Butter Cream Frosting** (page 9)
Large sprinkle-looking candy
Corrugated cardboard

METHOD

1. Grease and flour 3 9-inch round cake pans. Divide the batter evenly among the pans. Bake for 20 to 25 minutes, until a toothpick inserted in the center comes out clean.

2. Place one layer of your giant cupcake on a plate and spread some frosting on top. Place the second layer on top of the first and frost the top. Place the third layer on top and frost the top of this layer. If the cake does not have a natural dome shape to it, pile a little frosting in the center to give it that shape. Sprinkle the candies on top of the giant cupcake.

3. Measure the height of your cupcake. To make the cupcake's giant paper lining, trim the corrugated cardboard to the height of your cake minus 1 to 2 inches, so that you can see a bit of the cake peeking above the liner. Wrap the cardboard around your cupcake, cutting it where the ends meet. Attach the ends with a little bit of tape, or use a dab of frosting as glue.

This oversized cupcake is big enough for an entire birthday party.

> I bet the eskimos who live in these igloos feel warm and cozy behind the bricks of peppermint frosting.

Cupcake Igloos

INGREDIENTS

1 recipe batter for **Chocolate Cupcakes** (page 6)
1 tablespoon **peppermint extract**
1 recipe **Vanilla Butter Cream Frosting** (page 9)
20 **large marshmallows**

METHOD

1. Grease and flour cupcake tins. Fill the tins two-thirds full with batter and bake the cupcakes as directed in the recipe.

2. Add the peppermint extract to the frosting and mix well. Frost each cupcake (top and sides). If the cupcakes don't have natural domes on top, put a little more frosting on the centers to make them more igloo shaped. Use a toothpick or a small knife to draw brick shapes radiating from the center, to resemble the ice bricks of an igloo. It's fine if you can see the cake through the lines you are drawing; it will help define the brick shapes.

If the frosting is too soft to work with, refrigerate the frosted cupcakes for an hour and then draw the bricks.

3. Place the "igloos" on a serving plate, or plates. Using a small sharp knife, cut one edge off of a marshmallow to make a flat side. Place the marshmallow on the plate next to the cupcake, flat side down, and press it into the frosting to make the entrance to the igloo. Continue with the rest of the marshmallows, running the knife under hot water occasionally to make cutting the marshmallows easier.

These are good to make on a really hot summer day to remind you of a cooler place.

Mini-cupcake tins
Small gold foil cupcake liners (available at cake or candy decorating stores)
1 recipe batter for **White Cupcakes** (page 8)
1 recipe **Vanilla Butter Cream Frosting** (page 9)
White pearlescent powder (available at cake decorating stores)
Small clean **paintbrush**
Long needle (longer than the width of a mini-cupcake; also make sure that the eye is wide enough for your thread)
Embroidery thread or **string**

Who would have thought that cupcakes could make such an elegant accessory?

1. Line the cupcake tins with the liners. Use a small spoon to fill the tins two-thirds full with the batter. Bake for 10 minutes, until the top of a cupcake springs back when touched.

2. Frost the cupcakes. Refrigerate the "pearls" for at least 15 minutes so the frosting sets. Remove from the fridge and brush pearlescent powder on each little pearl.

3. Cut a long (about 2½ feet) piece of thread. Thread the needle and tie a knot at one end. Carefully pierce a cupcake through the center of its gold liner. Tie another knot next to the cupcake. Now skip 2 inches and tie another knot. Thread another cupcake and continue tying knots and threading cupcakes until you have reached the desired length of your lovely necklace. Tie the ends together. Continue until you have made enough pearl necklaces to fill a treasure chest!

These tasty necklaces would be lovely to serve to the ladies at a fancy luncheon or tea. Or you could color the frosting purple, gold, and green and make them for Mardi Gras.

Cupcake Pearls

Be careful when biting into this ocean of blue frosting waves—the beast of the deep could be lurking in the cupcake below.

Cupcake Sharks

INGREDIENTS

Blue paper cupcake liners

1 recipe **batter for any cupcake** (Red Velvet would be good—the color makes me think of sharks!)

1 recipe **Candy Dough** (page 6)

Black food coloring

Small clean **paintbrush**

1 recipe **Vanilla Butter Cream Frosting** (page 9)

Blue food coloring

METHOD

1. Line cupcake tins with the liners. Fill the tins two-thirds full with the batter and bake the cupcakes as directed in the recipe.

2. Mold a piece of the Candy Dough into a triangle shape about $1\frac{1}{2}$ inches tall and about 1 inch wide. The thickness could be around $\frac{1}{2}$ inch at the center of the triangle, but slightly thinner along the edges. Make the top point of the triangle bend back facing one side. Make about 20 fins (as many as you have cupcakes). Wipe a little black food coloring on each one.

3. Reserve a couple spoonfuls of the frosting and set aside for whitecaps for the waves. Tint the remaining frosting blue like the ocean. Frost the cupcakes, pulling some of the frosting upward to make waves in your ocean. With a toothpick, decorate your waves with some white frosting to make whitecaps and sea foam. Place your shark fins in the waves.

How about making these for a beach or pool party? Yikes!

48

Cupcake Village

Imagine the cute people who live in these tiny houses and the wild parties they must throw!

INGREDIENTS

1 recipe **batter for any cupcake**
1 recipe **Vanilla** or **Chocolate Butter Cream Frosting** (page 9)
1 recipe **Royal Icing** (page 9)
Food coloring
Assorted **cookies** and **candies***
Pastry bag and **tips** (optional)

METHOD

1. Place paper liners in some of the cupcake tins. Grease and flour the remaining tins (so that you have some different-looking houses). Fill the liners and tins two-thirds full with the batter and bake them as directed in the recipe.

2. Let this be an art project as well as a really special dessert. Tint some of the Butter Cream Frosting and some of the Royal Icing with food coloring, if you wish. Spread out the cookies and candy on a table or workspace so that you can see all of your building supplies.

3. Start construction on your houses. Frost entire cupcakes (without liners) and place a roof and a door in the frosting. Let cupcake liners act as walls and just frost the tops to stick a cookie roof or candy shingles on top. "Glue" doors and windows on liners or unfrosted cupcakes with a bit of Royal Icing. Also use icing to stick doorknobs onto doors. Use a pastry bag and tiny round tip to pipe vines or icing windows and doors onto the houses, if you wish.

*When choosing candy and cookies, let your imagination really run wild. Remember, this is your village and you're the builder! Stand in the candy and cookie aisle and look at everything as if you were at the hardware store. Here are some tips: Flat square or rectangle cookies make good roofs. Small rectangular candies (like chocolate bars that come in sections) make good doors. Little square candies or sliced jelly beans would make good windows. Small round candies make good shingles on a roof. Dragees (small round silver-coated candies) make good doorknobs. Ice cream cones make good roofs for gnomes' homes.

For serving, make a village on a big tray or on a table. You could use candy rocks (available at candy stores) for landscaping, or chocolate cookie crumb dirt on the ground of your village, or light brown sugar for sand if it's a desert town. Make pathways or streets or fences with square cookies or graham crackers. This is a good alternative to a gingerbread house for the holidays, too!

1 recipe batter for **White Cupcakes** (page 8)
1 recipe **Fluffy Frosting** (page 9)
20 **canned apricot halves**, drained

METHOD

1. Line cupcake tins with paper or foil liners.
Fill the liners a little more than three-quarters
full with the batter and bake the cupcakes
as directed in the recipe.

2. Frost the cupcakes. You can be sort of messy
about this, because if you have curvy edges
instead of perfect circles, the cupcakes will look
more like eggs. Place an apricot half on each
cupcake to make the "yolk." Continue with the
remaining cupcakes.

Serve these with coffee and orange juice
for an extra-special birthday breakfast.

Egg Cupcakes

Cleanup on aisle three!

Eyeball Cupcakes

INGREDIENTS

White paper cupcake liners
1 recipe batter for **White Cupcakes**
(page 8)
1 recipe **Vanilla Butter Cream Frosting**
(page 9)
Red food coloring
Pastry bag and **small round tip**
Small black jelly beans
**Round candies with hole in
the middle**

METHOD

1. Line cupcake tins with the liners. Fill the tins two-thirds full with the batter and bake the cupcakes as directed in the recipe.

2. Frost the cupcakes, reserving some of the frosting. Pile the frosting up a little in the center to make a sort of domed shape, more like an eyeball. To make the surface smooth, dip a butter or frosting/palette knife in hot water and smooth it over the top of the frosting.

3. Tint the remaining frosting bright red with the food coloring. Using the pastry bag, pipe the red frosting on the tops of the cupcake in vein patterns. Make the veins radiate from the center of the cupcake to make the bloodshot quality more realistic. Cut the jelly beans in half. Place a jelly bean half into the circle of the round candy. Now you have an iris and a pupil. Place this in the center of a cupcake. Continue with the rest of the eyeballs.

Make these visionary cupcakes to celebrate getting your first pair of glasses.

Maybe these cupcakes can help you catch up on all that reading you need to do.

Hamburger Cupcakes

These cupcakes will leave your friends asking, "Where's the beef?"

INGREDIENTS

1 recipe batter for **White Cupcakes** (page 8)
½ recipe batter for **Chocolate Cupcakes** (page 6)

METHOD

1. Grease and flour cupcake tins. Fill the tins two-thirds full with the batter and bake the cupcakes as directed in the recipes.

2. Slice off the tops of all the cupcakes and set aside. (You will not need the bases of the Chocolate Cupcakes, so you can munch on them or use them for another project.)

3. Slice a few of the bases of the White Cupcakes into ½-inch slices (approximately 10 slices total) and set aside.

Burger Fixin's Frosting

INGREDIENTS

1 recipe **Vanilla Butter Cream Frosting** (page 9)
Red and **green food coloring**
Sesame seeds

METHOD

1. Separate the frosting equally into two mixing bowls. With the food coloring, make one bowl of green and one bowl of red frosting.

2. Place one White Cupcake top on a flat surface (rounded side down). Now you have a hamburger bun bottom.

3. Place one chocolate top (rounded side up) on top of the bottom half of the bun to make the burger.

4. Spread a little green frosting on the burger to make the lettuce.

5. Frost one of the White Cupcake slices with red frosting to make a tomato. Place the tomato on top of the lettuce.

6. Place a second White Cupcake top (rounded side up) on the tomato to make the top of the bun. Sprinkle with sesame seeds.

7. Continue with the rest of the cupcakes.

A yummy dessert for a backyard cookout.

Makes 10 hamburgers.

Yellow paper or **gold foil cupcake liners**
1 recipe batter for **Chocolate-Caramel Cupcakes** (page 7)
1 recipe **Vanilla Butter Cream Frosting** (page 9)
Dark blue and **yellow food coloring**
½ (12-ounce) package **premade rolled fondant** (available at specialty pastry stores or online)
Powdered sugar
Yellow decorating sugar

METHOD

1. Line cupcake tins with the liners. Fill the liners two-thirds full with the batter and bake the cupcakes as directed in the recipe.

2. Tint the frosting midnight blue, the color of the night sky, with food coloring.

3. Knead a few drops of yellow food coloring into the fondant to tint it the color of a glowing star. Sprinkle a little powdered sugar on a work surface. Place the fondant on the powdered sugar and press it down to make the top of the fondant sort of flat. Sprinkle the yellow decorating sugar on the fondant. With a rolling pin, roll the fondant out to about ¼ inch thick. Rolling the fondant will also press the sugar into the fondant to make it sparkly (like a star!). With a small sharp knife, cut star shapes out of the fondant. Frost the cupcakes with the blue frosting and press a shiny star on each cupcake top.

Arrange these cupcakes in a constellation shape. You can even make a star field background for your cupcakes by drawing galaxies and planets on a piece of blue or black posterboard with a light-colored pencil.

These cosmic cupcakes are totally far out!

Intergalactic Cupcakes

Mushroom Cupcakes

When the snow has melted, the birds are chirping, and the spring rains have started to clear, look for these cheerful fungi in the magic forest.

1 recipe batter for **White Cupcakes** (page 8)
1 recipe **Vanilla Butter Cream Frosting** (page 9)
Red food coloring
Small round white candies

METHOD

1. Line cupcake tins with paper liners. Fill the tins a little more than three-quarters full (so they will have bigger tops on them, making them look more like mushrooms) and bake the cupcakes as directed in the recipe. Once the cupcakes are cool, remove the liners. This will make the stems of the mushrooms smaller and more realistic.

2. Tint the frosting bright red with the food coloring. Frost the cupcakes. Randomly apply the candies to the red frosting to make spots on the mushrooms.

Take these cupcakes when hiking (or mushroom picking!) in the woods.

Yellow paper cupcake liners
Glass marbles or small balls of **tinfoil**
1 recipe batter for **Peanut Butter Cupcakes** (page 8)
1 recipe **Vanilla Butter Cream Frosting,**
using 2 tablespoons **butter** and 1 cup **peanut**
butter in place of the ½ cup butter, plus three
tablespoons **milk** (page 9)
Pastry bag and **small round tip** (#4 works best)

METHOD

1. Line cupcake tin with the paper liners. Fill the tins half full with the batter. Place 2 marbles or marble-sized balls of tinfoil between each liner and the tin on opposing sides. This will make two indentations so that your cupcake will bake in a peanut shape. Bake the cupcakes as directed in the recipe. If you are using marbles, be careful when removing the cupcakes from the tins because the marbles will be very hot.

2. Frost the cupcakes. Using the pastry bag, pipe some of the frosting in a crosshatch pattern on top.

These cupcakes are perfect to serve at a circus- or baseball-themed party.

Your friends and family will go nuts for these peanutty treats.

Peanut Cupcakes

Peppermint Cupcakes

INGREDIENTS

1 recipe batter for **White Cupcakes** (page 8)

2 recipes **Royal Icing**, using

1 teaspoon **peppermint extract** in place of the lemon juice (page 9)

Red food coloring pen, or **red food coloring** and **small clean paintbrush**

METHOD

1. Grease and flour cupcake tins. Fill the tins half full with the batter and bake the cupcakes as directed in the recipe.

2. If the icing is too thick to spread easily, add 1 teaspoon water and mix well. Be careful not to make the icing too watery, as it will take too long to set. Put the cupcakes on a wire rack with a piece of waxed paper on a cookie sheet underneath. Spoon the icing on the cupcakes, letting it drip down the sides. Periodically, scrape the icing back into the bowl so you don't waste too much. Tilt the metal rack to make sure icing gets on the sides of the cupcakes. This will be messy, but it's worth it!

3. Let the cupcakes set on the wire rack or waxed paper until the icing is very hard. With the red food coloring pen, or a small brush dipped into a dish of food coloring, draw a spiral pattern onto the tops of the cupcakes, radiating from the center. Continue the spiral stripes down the sides of the cupcakes.

Here's a creative way to serve these (plus it keeps the cupcakes covered and fresh): Once the cupcakes have completely set, loosely wrap cellophane around them. Pinch one end of the cellophane together and tie it with a piece of clear plastic string. Do the same with the other end.

Piña Colada Cupcakes

A Hawaiian breeze is blowing, the tiki torches are blazing, and everyone is toasting summer by clinking the glasses of their festive Piña Colada Cupcakes.

INGREDIENTS

1 recipe batter for **Pineapple Cupcakes** (page 8)
1 recipe **Cream Cheese Frosting** (page 9)
2 cups **sweetened shredded coconut**
6 **tall drinking glasses**
Pastry bag (optional)
Pineapple wedges and **cherries**, for garnish (optional)

METHOD

1. Grease and flour tops and sides of cupcake tins. Fill the tins half full with the batter and bake the cupcakes as directed in the recipe. If you need to, when the cupcakes are completely cool, trim the edges of your cupcakes with a serrated knife so they will fit in the glasses.

2. Place 1 cupcake in a tall glass. Using a small spoon or a pastry bag, cover the top of the cupcake with frosting. Place another cupcake in the glass and put some more frosting on top. Add another cupcake (if it will fit in your glass). Place some more frosting on top. Sprinkle a handful of coconut on top of the frosting. Garnish with a pineapple wedge and cherry, if you like. Repeat with the remaining cupcakes and glasses.

How about hosting a tropical party in the middle of winter? Turn up the heat, put on a Hawaiian shirt, and mix up a batch of these fun tropical drinks.

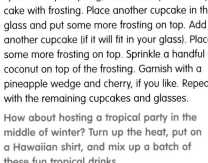

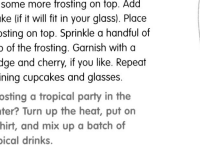

1 recipe batter for **White Cupcakes**
(page 8)

1 recipe **Vanilla Butter Cream Frosting**
(page 9)

Food coloring

1 tube each of **black, red, yellow,** and
white decorating icing with small tip

METHOD

1. Line cupcake tins with the liners.
Fill the liners three-quarters full with
the batter and bake the cupcakes
as directed in the recipe.

2. Using food coloring, mix colors
of frosting for the balls you like the
most (white for baseballs, yellow
for tennis balls, orange for basket-
balls).

3. Frost the cupcakes.

4. Using the decorating icing tubes,
apply lines to decorate the balls.

These are great for a sports-
themed party or to celebrate
winning a big game.

Score one for the team with
these sporty treats. They're
a big hit on game day.

Play-Off
Cupcakes

Flowers

INGREDIENTS

1 recipe batter for **Honey Cupcakes** (page 7)

METHOD

Line cupcake tins with the liners. Fill the liners three-quarters full with the batter and bake the cupcakes as directed in the recipe.

Frosting

INGREDIENTS

1 recipe **Vanilla Butter Cream Frosting** colored with the **food coloring** of your choice (page 9)
2 tablespoons **clear honey**
Small candy sprinkles in color of your choice
Round disc candies (like Necco Wafers) in colors of your choice (make sure these aren't too heavy, so they won't fall off)

METHOD

1. Frost the cupcakes thickly. Pour candy sprinkles into a small bowl and place the cupcakes upside down into the sprinkles to cover the frosting.

2. Place round disc candies around the outside edge of the cupcakes to make petals.

Bees

INGREDIENTS

1 recipe **Candy Dough** (page 6)
Yellow and **black food coloring**
icing glue (¼ cup **powdered sugar** and 1 teaspoon **water** mixed together)
Small candies for eyes, antennae and mouths
Sliced almonds for wings
Toothpicks

METHOD

1. Make the Candy Dough as directed in the recipe.

2. Split off two-thirds of the candy dough. Add a few drops of yellow food coloring and knead to color the candy dough. Knead in a few drops of black food coloring to the remaining candy dough.

3. Roll the yellow candy into small egg shapes about 1 inch long. Roll the black candy into a thin sheet. Cut it into rectangular strips about ½-inch wide and 2 inches long. Wrap each yellow egg with a black strip. You can also paint on black stripes with food coloring.

4. Using a little bit of icing glue, attach the bees' wings and faces using the almonds and small candies.

5. Place bees on toothpicks and insert into cupcakes. Make sure you tell your guests that they need to remove the toothpicks!

If you don't have time to make Candy Dough for the bees, you can also use premade fondant. Or paint yellow jelly beans with stripes of black food coloring. Serve these springtime cupcakes at an outdoor garden party.

> What bee could resist pollinating a flower as tasty as this?

Pollination Cupcakes

Savory Cupcakes

Cupcake

INGREDIENTS

¾ cup **yellow cornmeal**

1 cup **all-purpose flour**

1½ teaspoons **baking powder**

⅓ cup **sugar**

1 teaspoon **salt**

2 **eggs**

1 cup **whole milk**

4 tablespoons **unsalted butter,** melted

Frosting

INGREDIENTS

1 cup **fresh basil leaves**

1 clove **garlic**

¼ cup **pine nuts**

½ cup **olive oil**

Salt and **pepper**

1½ cups **cream cheese**

12 **cherry tomatoes**

METHOD

1. Preheat the oven to 350° F. Place paper liners in cupcake tins.

2. Sift the cornmeal, flour, baking powder, sugar, and salt together into a large mixing bowl.

3. In another bowl, beat the eggs together with the milk and butter. Add the milk mixture to the flour mixture and stir to combine.

4. Pour the batter into the cupcake liners two-thirds full. Bake for 18 to 20 minutes until golden brown.

5. In a blender or food processor, blend the basil, garlic, and pine nuts together. Slowly add the oil and blend until smooth. Season the pesto with salt and pepper to taste. Mix pesto with the cream cheese and use it to frost the cupcakes. Place a cherry tomato on top of each.

These are funny to serve on April Fool's Day. Or make them for your friend who doesn't have a sweet tooth.

Clare's Cupcake Bakery®
12.44 Sweet Street
Sugartown, La

Spaghetti and Cupcakes

Spaghetti and meatballs for dessert? Mama Mia!

INGREDIENTS

1 recipe batter for **Chocolate Cupcakes** (page 6)
Pastry bag and **medium (spaghetti-sized) tip**
2 recipes **Vanilla Butter Cream Frosting** (page 9)
1 (20-ounce) container **red fruit jam**, in a squeezable bottle

METHOD

1. Grease and flour cupcake tins. Fill the tins two-thirds full with the batter and bake the cupcakes as directed in the recipe.

2. Using the pastry bag, pipe frosting on a plate, making a mound of squiggly frosting.

3. Squeeze some jam "marinara sauce" onto the "spaghetti."

4. Place chocolate cupcake "meatballs" on the spaghetti.

These are also good to serve on April Fool's Day. You can make small individual plates of spaghetti for your guests, or one big serving platter. Feel free to make more Vanilla Butter Cream spaghetti if you want your dish to be piled high.

Sushi Cupcakes

Given as a gift in a bento box, these exotic sweets are considered a sign of thoughtfulness and respect.

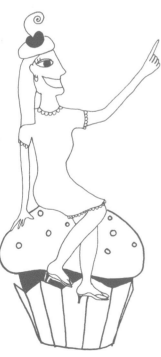

Cupcake

INGREDIENTS

1 recipe batter for **White Cupcakes** (page 8)

METHOD

Grease and flour cupcake tins. Fill the tins three-quarters full with the batter and bake the cupcakes as directed in the recipe.

Frosting

INGREDIENTS

1½ cups **sour cream**
¾ teaspoon **vanilla extract**
4½ cups **shredded coconut**
¾ cup **powdered sugar**, sifted

METHOD

1. In a medium mixing bowl, combine the sour cream, vanilla, and coconut.

2. Add the powdered sugar and mix thoroughly.

2. Using a butter knife, spread the frosting over the tops of the cupcakes.

Decoration

INGREDIENTS

8 **green Fruit Roll-Ups snacks**
Assorted candies (jelly beans, gummy worms, gummy fish)
Dried papaya and **mangoes**

METHOD

1. Trim the Fruit Roll-Ups to the height of the cupcakes. Wrap one fruit roll around the side of each cupcake.

3. Arrange the dried papaya and candies on the tops of the cupcakes.

4. Serve the dried mangoes on the side to resemble ginger.

Make your favorite type of sushi cupcakes by using different candy toppings. For a Japanese-themed party, create a whole sushi platter.

Volcano Cupcakes

Run for your life, or you might get swept away in the red frosting lava of this cupcake volcano!

INGREDIENTS

1 recipe batter for **Chocolate Cupcakes** (page 6)
1 recipe **White Ganache** (page 8)
Red food coloring
1 (10-ounce) bag **candy corn**

METHOD

1. Grease and flour cupcake tins. Fill the tins two-thirds full with the batter and bake the cupcakes as directed in the recipe.

2. When the cupcakes are completely cooled, place them upside down on plates or a serving tray. With a small serrated knife, carve out a little caldera (cone-shaped hole) in the top of each "volcano."

3. Tint the ganache with food coloring to make it the color of molten lava. Spoon it over the tops of the volcanoes, add a few pieces of candy corn for flames, and run like crazy!

Spread chocolate cookie crumbs on a tray and place your chocolate cupcakes on the "dirt" before you pour the lava frosting on them. You could put little model trees, houses, and people in your cupcake diorama, too.

Published by

MELCHER MEDIA

Melcher Media, Inc.
124 West 13th Street
New York, NY 10011
www.melcher.com

Publisher: Charles Melcher
Editor in Chief: Duncan Bock
Project Editors: Lia Ronnen and Megan Worman
Publishing Manager: Bonnie Eldon
Production Director: Andrea Hirsh
Editorial Assistant: Lauren Nathan

Design by Empire Design Studio

Pollination Cupcakes and Buttons and Thread Cupcakes
photographed by James Chinlund

Acknowledgments

A huge cupcake that looks like my heart goes to my love, James Chinlund, for helping me bake my dream.

A truck-full of cupcakes that look like bumblebees goes to Eric Staudenmaier. You are like sugar to work with, and I appreciate your photographic talent and knowledge so so so much.

A cornucopia of cupcakes in the most amazing color palette ever goes to Gary Tooth, whose graphic design makes me smile my head off.

Grocery bags filled with cupcakes—hopefully frosted as lovely as she can frost them—go to Lisa Barnet for her amazingly creative cupcake styling and all of her hard work.

Buckets of cupcakes go to everyone at Melcher Media.

A giant cupcake goes to Charles Melcher for being like Willy Wonka in his faith and trust in cupcakes.

A pile of cupcakes with really good chocolate sprinkles goes to Duncan Bock for having supersharp ideas and being an extremely smart, fun, and understanding editor. I appreciate your brain and our friendship.

A shopping bag full of sparkly and fashionable cupcakes goes to Lia Ronnen for her creativity, sense of humor, and enthusiasm.

A big box of especially delicious and fresh cupcakes goes to Megan Worman for her good ideas, patience, and diligence.

A tray of really delicious chocolate cupcakes goes to my friend Samantha Gore for being such a talented, supportive, and helpful friend.

Individual and especially beautiful cupcakes go to my friends for helping me bake it happen: Roz Music, Heather Levine, Crystal Meers, April Napier, Cayce and Todd Cole, Dee Dee Gordon, Phil Morrison, and Hayley and Mike Simpson.

A bunch of red velvet cupcakes that taste like big hugs go to my family for letting me be who I am. Thanks Mom, Dad, Libby, Paul, Marie, Granny, Caroline, Steve, and Zep.

A special pink cupcake goes to Connie Collins for the title that makes me laugh.

Melcher Media would like to thank David E. Brown, Suzanne Fass, Liana Fredley, Melinda Gale, Julia Joern, John Meils, Lindsey Stanbery, Danielle Svetcov, Shoshana Thaler, Shān Willis, and Western Laser Graphics.